How to Climb™ Series

How to
Rappel!

Craig Luebben

D1114357

FALCON GUIDE®

GUILFORD, CONNECTICUT
HELENA, MONTANA
AN IMPRINT OF THE GLOBE PEQUOT PRESS

Cover photo by Craig Luebben
Inside photos by Craig Luebben unless otherwise noted

Library of Congress Cataloging-in-Publication Data is on file at the Library of Congress

ISBN-13: 978-1-56044-759-7
ISBN-10: 1-56044-759-1

Manufactured in the United States of America
First edition/Third printing

WARNING: CLIMBING IS A SPORT WHERE YOU MAY BE SERIOUSLY INJURED OR DIE

READ THIS BEFORE YOU USE THIS BOOK.

This is an instruction book for rock climbing and rappelling, sports which are inherently dangerous. You should not depend solely on information gleaned from this book for your personal safety. Your climbing safety depends on your own judgment based on competent instruction, experience, and a realistic assessment of your climbing ability.

There is no substitute for personal instruction in rappelling and climbing instruction is widely available. You should engage an instructor or guide to learn climbing safety techniques. If you misinterpret a concept expressed in this book, you may be killed or seriously injured as a result of the misunderstanding. Therefore, the information provided in this book should be used only to supplement competent personal instruction from a climbing instructor or guide. Even after you are proficient in climbing safely, occasional use of a climbing guide is a safe way to raise your climbing standard and learn advanced techniques.

There are no warranties, either expressed or implied, that this instruction book contains accurate and reliable information. There are no warranties as to fitness for a particular purpose or that this book is merchantable. Your use of this book indicates your assumption of the risk of death or serious injury as a result of climbing's risks and is an acknowledgement of your own sole responsibility for your climbing safety.

C O N T E N T S

Acknowledgments

Thanks to John Bicknell and Ed Crothers, owners of Colorado Mountain School, one of America's premier mountain guide services, for reviewing this book and offering many valuable suggestions. Thanks also to Joe Josephson, who created the initial outline and contributed many ideas on rappelling.

Much appreciation goes to my great models who suffered through my sour moods when re-shooting certain sequences for the *third* time, or when the deadline was looming like a guillotine: Jen Barrientos, Steph Davis, Carol Adair, Joe Corsini, and Silvia Luebben.

Finally, thanks to the following companies for contributing gear: Trango, Misty Mountain Threadworks, Five Ten, Petzel, Stonewear Designs, and Sterling Ropes.

Foreword

My introduction to technical climbing was by way of rappelling at age fourteen. We bought a seventy-foot piece of 9-millimeter rope and wore it out rappelling off the outdoor handball courts at our junior high school. In time, rappelling for me became only a tool for descending from climbs.

Rappelling is used in many endeavors, though: spelunking, canyoneering, urban and wilderness rescue, military maneuvers, window washing, bird research, tree climbing, rock and ice climbing, and mountaineering. Many people consider rappelling a sport unto itself. Though this book is written from the climbing/mountaineering perspective, the principles covered are relevant to all disciplines of rappelling.

Rappelling is serious business. It consistently ranks among the leading causes of climbing fatalities, according to *Accidents in North American Mountaineering*. Performed with care, you can make thousands of rappels without incident. Get careless, and your next rappel may be your last.

(opposite page)
Rappelling to descend from the West Buttress, Eldorado Canyon, Colorado.

The Standard Rappel

Ah, rappelling. You've got to love it and hate it. It's a great tool in the mountains, and it can even be fun, but sometimes it's the scariest part of the day. Rappelling sometimes means failure—you're doing it because the route was too hard, too dangerous, or a storm bouted you. At least you've got gravity on your side—unless you screw up.

After a climb, it's often faster, safer, and more convenient to get back to the ground by rappelling. Sometimes rappelling is the only way down. Rappelling forces total reliance on your equipment. Everything must be rigged perfectly—one mistake and you're history. Often rappelling comes at the end of a long day or in the face of miserable weather, when your guard might be down. Well, don't let that guard down—ever. Safe rappelling demands constant attention to detail, and you must *always* double-check every link in the safety chain before rappelling.

This chapter briefly describes the basic steps involved in rappelling and lists the page number where each step is covered in detail.

SINGLE-PITCH RAPPEL

If you can make it to the ground in one rappel, it's a "single-pitch" rappel. Let's say two rappellers are on top of a seventy-foot cliff. They set up a bombproof anchor system (page 11). If the anchors are "fixed" (permanently left in place), they inspect and reinforce them, if necessary. Both rappellers clip into the anchors if it's an exposed rappel station (page 51).

If they're fixing the rope to be retrieved later, they tie one end into the anchors (page 14). If they'll be pulling the ropes down from below, they pass one rope through the anchors and tie it to another rope (page 14). If they only have one rope, they run the rope through the anchors and set the middle of the rope at the rappel point. They tie stopper knots in the free rope end(s) (page 29), yell, **"Rope!,"** and toss the rope(s) down (page 48).

One of them rigs his rappel device to the rope(s) (page 32), adds an autoblock backup (page 37), double-checks everything (page 37), and tucks away any long hair or loose clothing that might get stuck in the rappel device (page 44). He unclips from the anchors and transfers his weight to the rappel device. With his guide hand on the autoblock and brake hand below, he lets the rope slowly slide through the rappel device. Body facing the cliff, feet shoulder-width apart, legs perpendicular to the rock, torso bent at the waist, he descends at a controlled speed and "walks" down the wall (page 43). If he needs to stop, he locks up the autoblock. He watches for the end of the rope on his way

(opposite page)
Descending Independence Monument, Colorado National Monument.

Moses, Canyonlands National Park, Utah. The only way down is to rappel.

down. Once safely on the ground, he disconnects from the rope(s), and yells, **"Off rappel!"** He should now move away from the rappel line into an area that's safe from falling rocks or gear. He should yell, **"Clear!"** when he's safe.

His partner repeats the process, keeping the ropes free from any constrictions that might jam it. When she gets down, they pull the ropes (page 49)—if they're not fixed—and yell, **"Rope!"** just before the ropes tumble down.

MULTI-PITCH RAPPEL

A gorgeous drive through the desert, a few grueling pitches, and now you're on top of the stunning spire called Moses. There's only one sane way back down: rappel.

If descending requires more than a single rappel, you have a "multi-pitch" rappel. Multi-pitch rappelling requires many steps and an amazing number of decisions. Let's say two climbers have just finished a long route, and they're preparing to rappel the route back to the ground. They first inspect the soundness of the anchors and reinforce them if necessary (page 15), then clip into them with a cow's tail or a daisy chain (page 13). They pass one rope end through the anchor rappel point, and tie the rappel ropes together (page 26). They tie stopper knots in the ends of both ropes (page 29), yell, **"Rope!,"** and toss the ropes down (page 48). Both climbers make a mental note of which rope to pull when retrieving the ropes. They may clip their cow's tail into the rope that gets pulled to remember which one it is. This also prevents the ropes from twisting around each other, which could jam them.

The first rappeller, often the more experienced of the two, rigs her rappel device to the ropes and adds an autoblock safety backup (page 37). She double-checks her harness buckle, anchors, rappel device, locking carabiner, knot joining the ropes, and autoblock, then rappels. Along the way, she's careful that the rope doesn't run over sharp edges, she watches out for loose rocks, and she keeps looking for the next anchor station (page 48). If the terrain is ledgy, bushy, or less than vertical, she probably has to untangle and re-toss the ropes periodically as she rappels.

The first person down must be extremely careful not to rappel off the rope ends. If the ends are fixed with stopper knots, it's not possible to rappel off the rope—unless the rappeller is using a large figure-8 device and has not rigged the autoblock backup.

When the first rappeller arrives at the next anchor station, she checks the anchors, reinforces them if they are not bombproof, and re-rigs them if the rigging is messy. She then clips into the anchors, double-checks the clip-in, and clips the rappel lines into the anchors if the rappel above was diagonal or overhanging. She dismantles her rappel device and hollers, **"Off rappel!"** so her partner knows the rope is free.

The second rappeller rigs his rappel device, adds an autoblock backup, double-checks everything, and begins rappelling. He's careful that the ropes remain untwisted above him, and that the rope doesn't lay in any cracks that might cause it to get stuck. While waiting for the second rappeller to come down, the first rappeller passes the rope to be pulled through the next rappel point and ties a new stopper knot in its end. When the second rappeller arrives at the anchor station, he clips in and double-checks his clip-in. He dismantles his rappel device, while keeping a hold of the ropes.

The rappellers then remove the stopper knot from the free rope. One person pulls the ropes down (page 49), while the other feeds the rope through the new anchor point and ensures that no knots or twists pass up the rope being pulled through the anchors, lest it get stuck. Both climbers are vigilant to never drop the ropes and lose them, an embarrassing and possibly life-threatening mistake.

When pulling the ropes, just before they come free from the top anchor, one (or both) rappeller yells, **"Rope!"** Whoever's pulling the rope whips it outward, away from the rock. After the rope falls, they re-gather it, tie a stopper knot in the end, yell, **"Rope!"** again, and toss it for the next rappel. Once the ropes are set for the next rappel, with the knot at the anchors, the team repeats the procedure, over and over, until they reach the ground.

Rappel Anchors

ANCHORS

Every rappel starts with finding or building a sound anchor system. Rappel stations should have at least two or three bombproof anchors, rigged to create a single, equalized rappel point. If the anchors are less than bomber, back them up or replace them. Don't get in the sloppy habit of blindly trusting fixed gear such as bolts and pitons. Inspect the anchors, webbing, and surrounding rock thoroughly. Just because someone else rappelled from them doesn't mean they're good anchors. Anchor failure has killed many climbers and rappellers. John Long's books *Climbing Anchors* and *More Climbing Anchors*, also in Falcon's How to Rock Climb series, cover anchors and anchor systems in detail.

Bolts

Bolts can be your best friends or your worst nightmares. It's important to learn to identify them, so you know how much to

One-quarter, ⅜- and ½-inch diameter Rawl stud bolts. Don't expect the ¼-inch jobs to hold a fall, although they might. One-quarter-inch bolts should be replaced at every opportunity. The two bigger sizes are bomber, if the rock and the placement are good.

A relic from the old days. You still find these Star Dryvn bolts occasionally. To set these bolts, you drive an aluminum nail into the steel sleeves. A lead flange on the bottom of the sleeves expands to hold the bolt in place. Don't trust them too much, especially the tiny, ¼-inch models.

One-quarter-inch buttonhead. You can still find lots of these in some climbing areas. They're not safe and should be replaced.

(opposite page) To rappel, you need solid anchors, and all the rigging must be correct—one mistake may be your last.

Ah, now we're talking. A ½-inch Rawl 5-piece is as bomber as it gets. When you see such a bolt head, it's probably a good anchor.

A solid, ⅜-inch Rawl stud.

trust a given bolt. Old ¼-inch bolts, usually 1 to 1 ½ inches deep, are unsafe. Unfortunately, many rappel anchors still consist of ¼-inch bolts. These should be replaced or backed up at every opportunity.

Anchor bolts should be at least ⅜ inch in diameter and 3 inches deep, and they should fit tightly in their holes. Equalizing two or three good bolts creates a convenient, sound rappel anchor.

Pitons

Cast an eye of suspicion on every fixed piton you find. Is it rusty, shallow in its placement, or poorly oriented to hold a load? Is it old, cracked, or loose? Some pitons are bomber, others are worthless. It's up to you to decide.

Thermal expansion of the rock, caused by hot days and cold nights, can loosen pitons over time. It's good to test fixed pitons

lightly with a hammer, though most free climbers and rappellers don't carry a hammer. Don't abuse pitons when testing them with a hammer; you can damage them. Lacking a hammer, visually inspect fixed pins. Don't trust the piton unless it's relatively new and well placed. Even then, back up fixed pins whenever you can.

It's often hard to judge fixed pitons unless you have a hammer.

Nuts

Wired and slung nuts make great rappel anchors, if they're buried into bomber constrictions in good rock. Avoid nut placements that can pull free with an outward tug. Nuts are fairly cheap, so you can leave them as rappel anchors without too much pain.

A good nut placement has constrictions preventing a downward **and** outward tug from dislodging the nut.

This placement has a good constriction against a downward pull, but a slight outward pull might jerk it free. Find a slightly deeper placement with a lip to prevent the nut from getting pulled outward, if you can.

Cams

The situation would have to be pretty bleak to justify leaving camming units as rappel anchors. However, you might use them to back up the fixed anchors until the last person rappels. The important principles for setting cams are: (1) point the stem in the direction of loading; (2) choose the right size unit so the cams are between 10 and 50 percent open (avoid the smallest 10 percent or biggest half of the expansion range); (3) make sure the opposite cams are evenly deployed (not offset); and (4) place the cam in solid rock.

If the cam has a rigid stem, avoid loading the stem over a rock edge, or it could bend or break. It's okay for cable stems to bend over edges, though the cables might get kinked under a heavy load. If so, check for frayed cables and bend them back into shape. A cam pushes outward twice as hard as you pull down, so don't place them behind loose blocks or detached flakes.

Here's a good cam placement in solid rock, with the cams slightly more than halfway closed.

This camming unit is too small for the crack, so the cams are almost fully extended. The next size unit fits much better.

The cams on this unit are offset—one cam is closed more than its opposing cam, which could cause the unit to pull out.

The rigid stem loaded over this edge could bend or break in a fall. Place the cam deeper in the crack, or use a unit with a flexible stem.

Trees

Trees make great rappel anchors, but they must be alive, well rooted, and stout. The roots must be anchored in rock cracks or deep soil, not just a few inches of dirt on a ledge. Even if fixed slings tell you that others have rappelled from the tree before, check it out. It's your life and your call. A climber in Valdez, Alaska, was rappelling the standard descent of a route while his partner remained clipped to their anchor, a tree. Suddenly, the anchor tree ripped out. The man who was rappelling dropped, and the weight pulled off his partner. Both fell to their deaths. It's possible the tree roots and soil were weakened by passing crampons.

On medium-size trees, tie the tree off close to the ground to minimize leverage and gain maximum strength. On huge trees, you might tie off a solid, thick, living branch a foot or more in diameter. Some rappels go off a single burly tree, but if it's less than massive, back up and equalize the tree with other anchors.

Occasionally, for a short rappel, you can simply pass your rope around a stout tree. This is usually avoided, though, because it can be hard to pull your rope from below, and repeated rope pulls will damage the tree. It's better to tie a pair of slings around the tree, add two rappel rings, and run the rappel rope through the rings.

A solid, living, well-rooted tree at least ten inches in diameter makes a quick, easy rappel anchor. It's best to sling the tree and pass the rope through the sling as shown. If you'll be rappelling a fixed rope, tie a figure-eight knot in one end of the rope and clip it to the slings with two carabiners. At least one of the carabiners should be locking.

Don't even think it! This tree is dead, and you may be, too, if you use it as a rappel anchor.

Natural Rock Features

The most satisfying rappel anchor is a natural rock feature—a horn, tunnel, flake, boulder, or chockstone that you tie off with cord or webbing. Natural protection is usually quick to place, and if you have to leave gear, it's the cheapest way to go. Like any anchor, the rock must be solid, and you need at least two good anchors. Many backcountry rappel stations consist of multiple slings around a single solid horn or through a tunnel. It's always your judgment call whether or not to trust the fixed anchors you find—you can never go wrong by adding a nut or two to back up fixed anchors.

When topping out on the Salathe Wall on El Capitan, Todd Skinner and Paul Piana were anchored to a huge boulder that was the standard belay anchor for many years. While Todd was jumarring the last pitch, the boulder came free, severing pieces of the rope and nearly killing them both. A single backup piton saved them.

A solid horn of rock can make a good natural anchor. The rock must be firmly embedded in the surrounding rocks, not a loose block sitting near an edge. Here, two loops of cord wrap around the block, and a double-strand loop of cord extends the anchors so the rope can be pulled down from below after the rappel. The overhand knot makes the extension cord redundant—if one strand cuts, the others still hold the weight.

You could just pass the rope directly around a very solid horn, but it could damage the rope, and you probably won't be able to pull the rope down from below because of too much friction.

A well-wedged chockstone can make an emergency rappel anchor. In this case it would be better if the right side of the chockstone made better contact with the wall. Back this anchor up, and if the chockstone is loose at all don't trust it. You might pull it down on yourself.

Though it's better to place a nut, you can tie a knot in webbing or cord and jam it in a crack to supplement your rappel anchors. Jammed knots can be decent if you make a good placement, but I'd never use them as the primary anchor.

Jammed knots can make emergency rappel backups, but they have to be placed in a very tight constriction. Don't trust them as the primary anchor.

You can vary the size of the knot to fit the crack.

Forces

The force on your rappel anchors is well below that of a climbing lead fall, but it can still be substantial—up to 1,000 pounds, with some bouncing on the rope. You can minimize the force by rappelling smoothly. Nonetheless, rappel anchors must be bomb-proof, or the rappel may go way faster than you bargained for—after the anchors rip out.

Many rappel anchors, including pitons, chocks, and bolts (especially old bolts or bolts placed in soft rock) are strong against a downward pull but not against an outward pull. Don't lean out on the anchors when starting a rappel. Instead, load the anchors downward.

RIGGING ANCHORS

All the anchors in the system should be equalized and rigged to create a single rappel point. An acronym developed by the American Mountain Guides Association—EARNEST—helps to remember the important concepts for building a rappel anchor.

E stands for *equalized*—all the anchors should share the load, to maximize the strength of the anchor system.

A stands for *angle*—the V-angle between the slings connecting the anchors should be less than 60 degrees. Doubling the V-angle to 120 degrees doubles the load on the anchors.

R means *redundant*—never rely on one anchor, one sling, or one rappel ring—always have backups.

NE refers to *no extension*—the anchors should be rigged so that if one anchor pops, you don't get slack in the system and shock load the remaining anchors.

S means *solid*—the individual anchors and the overall system must be absolutely bombproof.

T stands for *timely*—if you spend all day building your anchors, you won't get much climbing or rappelling done.

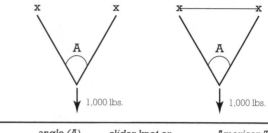

angle (A)	slider knot or independent slings (pounds)		American Triangle (pounds)
0°	500		707
30°	518	comfort	821
60°	577		1,000
90°	707	caution	1,306
120°	1000		1,932
150°	1932	danger	3,830
175°	11,463		22,920

If the anchor system is required to support 1,000 pounds, the figure shown in the table is the resulting force on each anchor.

Increasing or decreasing the load on the anchor system results in a proportional increase or decrease on each anchor.

The obtuse "V-angle" of 120 degrees in this rigging doubles the force on the anchors.

This American Triangle with a 60 degrees V-angle doubles the load on the anchors.

Clipping In

At any exposed belay or rappel anchors, the team should be clipped in. It's convenient to girth hitch a new sewn sling onto your harness belay loop or tie-in point to make a cow's tail, and clip it to the anchors with a locking carabiner. Clip into an equalized point between the anchors if possible. If not, at least clip into all the anchors.

When rappelling, clip the cow's tail to the side of your harness to keep it out of your way, or clip it to the rope you need to pull to retrieve the ropes after the rappel. Sometimes, it's nice to have two cow's tails, for clipping two chains or bolts at a fixed anchor.

Some climbers girth hitch a daisy chain to their harness for clipping the anchors. This works well, especially since you can easily adjust the length of the daisy, but it's heavier and more bulky than just a sling. Never clip a carabiner to adjacent loops in the daisy chain because if the stitches between the loops blow out, you'll have total failure of the daisy chain.

You can girth hitch a sling to your harness to make a cow's tail for clipping into the anchors.

A daisy chain, though more to carry, is even more handy because it has several loops for adjusting the length of your clip-in. Never clip more than one loop of the daisy into a carabiner.

Rigging Your Ropes

If you don't need to retrieve the rope from the bottom, you can "fix" it by tying or clipping it into the anchors with a figure-8 knot or equalizing figure-8 knot. With a fixed rope, you usually rappel on a single strand.

Ropes to be retrieved from below must pass through the anchor rings, with the middle of the rope set at the anchors. With one rope, though, you can rappel only half a rope length.

For a full-length rappel you need two ropes. Pass one rope through the rappel rings and tie the ropes together with a recommended rappel knot. Set the knot near the anchors. This gives you two equal-length rope strands for rappelling and retrieval, so you can rappel farther and leave less fixed gear. Most in-situ rappel routes require two ropes to reach the anchors.

1. Rappelling a fixed line tied off to the anchors with a figure-8 knot. Locking carabiners keep the rope secure.

2. This fixed rope is tied off with an equalizing figure-8, which distributes the load between the anchors.

3. Rappelling on a single rope to be retrieved from below. The rope has been fed through the fixed chain rings, with the rope's midpoint set right at the rings to create two equal-length rope strands for rappelling.

4. By tying two ropes together, you can rappel a full rope length and still retrieve the ropes from below.

Equalizing Figure-8 Knot

Chain or Ring Anchors

On many descent routes, anchor stations are fixed with permanent chains or rings. These are less ugly than webbing or cord, and they make descending quick and easy. Always inspect the anchors and rings for wear. If they look good, clip into them, and feed your rope through the rings for rappelling. It's best if the rigging equalizes the load on the anchors, but unfortunately, that's often not the case with fixed anchors.

These chains are fixed as a belay and rappel station. Fixed chains last much longer than slings, and they're visually less obtrusive than webbing. These chains have been painted camouflage colors to lessen their visual impact.

For rappelling, pass the rope through the bottom chain links of the two outside bolts. Going through the middle bolt here would cause impossible rope drag. You can still use the middle bolt to bolster the belay or as a rappel backup anchor.

Cold Shuts

Borrowed from the construction industry, cold shuts have been widely used as hangers for rock bolts because they are cheap. Cold shuts are not strong enough to be safe climbing anchors, unless they have been properly welded. With a good weld, cold shuts make a convenient anchor because you can pass the rope directly through them to rappel— no need to leave ugly slings or rappel rings. A pair of unwelded cold shuts is probably strong enough for a rappel anchor, but I definitely wouldn't climb above them, as the rope might slip out of the open "shut."

An open cold shut is a sketchy anchor because it's not closed around the rope, and it's not as strong as other anchors.

Rigging with Slings

If you're relying on fixed slings or cord left by previous parties, check out the knots, and inspect the entire length of the slings or cord. Nylon left fixed at anchor stations can suffer from rockfall damage, varmint gnawing, or ultraviolet degradation from solar rays. It's best if the slings have two rings, carabiners, or rapid links at the rappel point for easy rope retrieval. Without such rings, the rope may saw through the slings when you pull it down.

Far too often, the rigging at fixed rappel stations is a shambles—knots you've never seen, sun-bleached slings all twisted and tangled together. It's hard to figure out where to clip in, or if the load is equalized. If the rigging is messy, cut it away with a knife and re-tie it from scratch with new slings. If it's not too bad, you might be able to just add a sling and carabiner or link to get by. If there's only one fixed sling or rappel ring, add

This manky rappel station was found in Vinales, Cuba. The wide V-angle of the sling nearly doubles the force on these rusty old pitons. On the left, the rope is tied through two pitons so that only one of them holds weight and, if it fails, it shock loads the other. The rope is not redundant either, though if you know the history, of the rope or webbing and can visually see that it is in good condition, a single piece can suffice in a pinch.

Neither of these anchors is any good, and they're rigged with the hideous American Triangle. Trust anchors like this and you'll likely get down much quicker than you bargained for.

another. It's good to carry some knotted webbing slings for bolstering rappel stations.

Webbing or cord both work great for equalizing anchors. With ten or twelve feet, you can run the sling through both anchors and tie the sling into a loop. Then pull down two loops of sling in the direction of loading (straight down for a rappel) and tie an overhand, or figure-8, to create the rappel point. If the angle between the loops of sling is more than 60 degrees, use a longer sling.

Here's a clean rigging that shares the load between both anchors, and it requires only 5 to 7 feet of cord. The cord must be replaced periodically as the nylon becomes UV-degraded.

You can also tie each end of a five- or eight-foot piece of webbing (depending on the webbing thickness and anchor layout) into the two anchors with overhand knots. Then pull down the middle of the sling in the direction of loading and tie another overhand knot with the rappel rings inside to create the rappel point. However, this rappel point loop is not redundant, so unless you have a brand new cord or piece of webbing, leave two or more slings tied in this arrangement.

If you neglect the middle overhand knot and one anchor fails, your rope will come free, as it did for a team of three climbers on El Capitan in Yosemite Valley. They clipped a chain between two bolts for their anchor. Somehow, a haulbag dropped and

You can tie a separate sling to each anchor and adjust the lengths so that each anchor shares in holding the load.

Pass the tail of webbing through the hanger for padding if the hangers have sharp edges.

slammed onto the anchors. One bolt broke, their carabiners slid off the chain, and they fell a thousand feet. You can guess the outcome.

One of the safest and most simple ways to rig the anchor system involves tying a separate sling into each anchor and adjusting the length of each sling so all anchors share the load.

If the anchors aren't great, and there's no way to improve them, they should be perfectly equalized to increase the strength of the overall anchor system. The two methods described above do not spread the load equally, unless you tie the slings off to exactly the right lengths. To perfectly equalize two anchors, use the "magic X". Tie a sling through both anchors and pull down two loops. Twist one loop 180 degrees, creating the magic X, and place the rappel rings or carabiners at the bottom of the loops.

Without the X, if one anchor fails, your rappel ring will slide off the sling, and you'll lose your anchors. If you create the X and an anchor fails, you'll still be connected to the second anchor.

It is possible to rig the magic X on more than two anchors. Run the sling through all the anchors, pull down a loop for each anchor, and twist all but one of them 180 degrees. This does not give you a redundant sling, however, so use a brand-new sling or double up the slings.

1. Bad. This rigging puts all the force on one piton. If it fails, the other receives a shock load.

2. Bad. This setup shares the load between the pitons, but if one of them rips out, the ring slides off the sling and you have total anchor failure.

3. Twisting one of the webbing loops 180 degrees to create the "magic X" ensures that the ring will not slide off the webbing if one anchor blows out.

4. The magic X distributes the load equally between two anchors, even if the loading direction changes. You need two slings or strands of cord to make the rigging redundant.

1. The American Triangle increases the load on your anchors by making them pull against each other.

One lame rigging is the infamous American Triangle, where the sling makes a triangle between the anchors and the point of loading. This increases the force on the anchors by making them pull against each other. The American Triangle might be okay if the anchors are beefy, new ⅜- or ½-inch diameter bolts, but still, why put extra load on your anchors?

Rigging with a Cordelette

When equalizing three or four anchors, a cordelette provides a clean, single rappel point. Cordelettes are generally made from a

A cordelette works well for rigging climbing belay anchors as shown here.

The cordelette also works well for rigging rappel anchors. Pass the cord through all the anchors and tie it into a loop with a double fisherman's knot. Pull down the strands of cord between the anchors in the direction of loading and tie an overhand knot to join the three loops together. This makes the rigging redundant—if one loop cuts, the other two loops are unaffected.

A long piece of webbing can also be rigged like a cordelette.

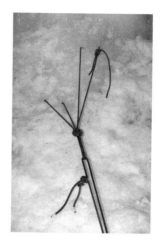

The cordelette rigging also works with only two anchors. Here the cord is doubled for extra strength.

Two ice tunnels threaded with a cordelette can make a strong rappel anchor in ice—if the ice is solid.

A web-o-lette is a length of webbing with loops sewn in both ends that works well for rigging anchors. You can use a web-o-lette to rig a rappel as shown here, though you'll be sad to leave this expensive sling.

A backup anchor is clipped to hold the rope if the main anchor fails. If the last rappeller down will be removing the backup, the fixed anchors should bear all the weight when the first people go down, so they get tested.

16- to 20-foot-long piece of 5.5- to 7-millimeter diameter accessory cord. Many brands of cord are available for use as cordelettes. If you use perlon, go with 6 millimeters or larger. My favorite cords are the high-strength 5- to 5.5-millimeter brands, such as Sterling HT or Maxim Tech cord, because they're strong, thin, and supple. In desperate times, you can cut off and use a piece of the climbing rope as a cordelette.

To rig the cordelette, pass the cord through all the anchors and tie it into a loop using a double grapevine knot. Pull down a strand of cord between each anchor, in the expected direction of loading, and tie the strands together with a figure-8 knot (or an overhand knot to save length). This knot isolates each loop, so if one loop cuts you won't have total failure. It also prevents shock loading should one anchor rip. If the direction of pull is different than expected, though, the cordelette will not provide equalization. If you're adding rappel rings, incorporate them into the cordelette rappel point as you tie it.

Another option for rigging that requires less cord is to tie one end of the sling or cord to an anchor with an overhand knot, pass the cord through the middle anchor, and tie the other end to the third anchor. Pull down two bights of rope between the anchors, toward the direction of loading, and tie a figure-8 knot in the four strands of cord to create the rappel point.

Unless the anchors are perfect, back up the rappel for everyone but the last climber down, with extra anchors set in a crack (if possible). Send all the heavy gear down with the first climbers. The backup gear shouldn't bear weight while the first rappellers go, so they "test" the anchors on their way down. Ideally, the lightest person goes last, though he may not be psyched about this position—it's his job to remove the backup anchors and rappel last. If the anchors are sketchy at all, leave the backup anchor in for the last person. It's far better to leave gear than have your anchors rip out and become a case story in *Accidents in North American Mountaineering*.

RAPPEL POINT

Rappel ropes are connected to the anchors through the rappel point. This is ideally a pair of metal links—rappel rings, carabiners, chain links, quick links, or rapid links. The rappel point should be equalized between all the anchors.

Be wary of aluminum rappel rings, which are commonly found at rappel stations. Especially in sandy environments, the rings erode as ropes are pulled through them. Always check the entire circumference of the rings for wear spots, and never rappel off a single

Fixed hardware prevents the need for constantly replacing rappel slings. The rappel point rings should be perpendicular to the rock.

Double rappel rings make a good rappel point. Make sure to inspect fixed rings before trusting them. Most that you'll find are aluminum, and they can wear out from repeated rope pulls, especially in the desert, where sand in the rope abrades the aluminum. These rings are titanium, which wear longer than aluminum rings.

This rope will become hopelessly kinked when you pull it through these rings because they are not oriented perpendicular to the rock.

This rapid link makes a nice rappel point, but it would be good if it were backed up.

A quick and dirty way to back up the rappel point is with a webbing loop. The loop should be long enough that it doesn't get weighted, so the rope runs through metal when you pull it down.

rappel ring—they should always be doubled or tripled. Sometimes a single rappel ring is backed up by a webbing loop, but it's better to have another ring or a carabiner for the backup.

Some rappel anchors have no ring—the rope runs directly through the webbing. This is safe enough for the first party or two that uses them, but the webbing will eventually be damaged as ropes are pulled down through it. Leaving webbing or cord with no rings is okay in a location where few others are likely to rappel (if you're off-route, or in a remote location, etc.), but popular rappel routes should definitely have rings, links, or carabiners. If no rings exist in an established rappel anchor, add some if you have them. The rope will pull more smoothly.

If no rings exist and you're rappelling with two ropes of significantly different diameters (1 millimeter or more in difference), the thicker rope must sit on the sling. Otherwise, as you rappel and the thin rope stretches, it will saw across the sling, possibly burning through it.

Extending the Anchors

When you have to bail off a climb, you can often use natural anchors to minimize the hardware that you leave. Here, a tied-off chockstone and a jammed knot make a cheap backoff anchor. Make sure the chockstone is bomber secure before trusting this setup.

If the rappel anchors are situated back from the lip of a ledge or cliff top, extend them with cord or webbing so the rappel point sits just below the lip, or it will be difficult to retrieve the ropes from below. Redundancy in the extension is critical—two or more independent sets of slings should run from the anchors to the rappel point, just below the lip. If the lip is sharp, use tape to protect the slings.

With the anchors extended, you may have to downclimb a bit to start rappelling. The slings make a good handhold while you climb down to where the rappel device takes your weight. The autoblock backup is your belayer here.

Bailing and Leaving Your Own Anchors

If you get nailed by a storm, climb off-route, drop critical gear, are moving too slowly, or find the route to be over your head, you may have to retreat. Usually, the best way down is to rappel the route, leaving your own hard-earned gear for rappel anchors if none are fixed. Use knowledge that you gathered on the way up to select rappel stations and minimize the amount of gear you abandon. Natural anchors should be your first choice so you only sacrifice webbing or cord. Since it's a retreat and not an established descent route, you might want to run the rope through the slings, rather than leaving carabiners or rings at each rappel. This will make the rope harder to pull down, though.

If you can't find fixed or natural anchors, the next-best choice is to leave wired nuts,

slung chocks, or—as a last resort—camming units. As precious as your gear is, don't be cheap and rappel on single or poor anchors. Hopefully, your life is worth more than a camming unit. Besides, the next party will love you if you leave a bunch of gear while retreating. If you're lucky, the next party will be you.

If you have many rappels, you may have to conserve gear at the anchors to be able to reach the ground. You'll be much happier if you have two ropes instead of just one, so you can rappel farther and minimize the number of stations where you need to leave gear.

Rope Management

ROPE USE AND CARE

"Ropes never break." Tell that to this guy: a large climber who was being lowered from a pitch. Just before he reached the ground, the rope broke—under body weight. He fell to the ground, but escaped serious injury. Lucky he wasn't eighty feet off the deck. Analysis of the rope showed traces of battery acid, probably picked up in the rat-infested trunk of a vagabond climber.

Treat your rope like your best friend: don't step on it, beware of sharp edges, and keep it away from chemicals. Carry the rope in a rope bag or tarp, and store it in a cool, dry, shaded place. Minimize exposure to the sun. If the rope gets excessively dirty, clean it in a tub, or better, with a rope washer that attaches to a garden hose.

It's nice to have middle marks on the rope when rigging single-rope rappels. Some ropes come with middle marks—tape or cord wrapped around the rope. These rarely last more than a few pitches before they wear off. The best system is a bi-colored rope where each half is a different color and pattern, making the middle obvious. If you don't have a bi-colored rope, you can mark the middle yourself; Marks-A-Lot, Sharpie, or Majic Marker pens are safe for making your own middle mark on a rope.

Ropes kink, foiling your rope management and wasting time. You can minimize kinking by unwinding new, factory-coiled ropes as if you're rolling them off a spool, rather than flaking them out. Also, avoid figure-8 rappel devices, Munter hitches, and the mountaineer's coil to keep your ropes from kinking.

When you can see the white of the core, it's time to retire the rope. Likewise, if you take a really hard lead fall, or if you find flat spots in the rope. Also, be wary of any rope older than four or five years. Choose a rope with kernmantle construction, which has a core to provide strength and a sheath to protect the core. Goldline ropes—relics from the past—are occasionally used for rappelling. They're less pleasant to manage, and you need leather gloves when rappelling on them. Goldline ropes are unsuitable for lead climbing.

Use ropes as they are intended to be used. For rappelling, you can use static ropes, which stretch little, or dynamic climbing ropes, which stretch to absorb energy in a lead climber's fall. NEVER lead on a static rope. When fixing lines for rope ascending or multiple rappels, use static rope, if possible, because it doesn't stretch and saw over edges as much as a bouncy lead rope.

TYPES OF ROPES

Dynamic Ropes

Rope designers build elasticity into dynamic ropes to control the deceleration rate of a falling climber. This limits the impact force on the climber, belayer, and anchors. The Union Internationale des Associations d'Alpinisme conducts severe drop tests on dynamic ropes before certifying them for lead climbing.

Single, Half, or Twin Ropes

Single ropes, marked by a one in a circle, are certified for a climber to lead on without another rope. Half ropes and twin ropes, designated with a ½ and a 2 in a circle, respectively, require two ropes for leading. It's a good idea to follow these guidelines for rappelling, as well. If you're going to rappel on one rope, it should be a single-rated rope. With half and twin ropes, you should rappel on two strands. If you're rappelling on a static line, it should be 10 millimeters or more in diameter.

Diameter and Length

Over the past twenty years, climbing ropes have become skinnier and longer. The standard rope length of 45 meters has grown to 50 or 60 meters, while the diameter of single ropes has shrunk from 11 millimeters to 10. Some lead ropes are as skinny as 9.4 millimeters. (Half ropes and twin ropes generally range from 8 to 9 millimeters.) A longer 60-meter rope means more to coil, carry, and manage, but the extra utility is often worth it. A long rope may allow you to rappel with one rope, so you can leave the second rope at home. With two long ropes, you can sometimes bypass one rappel station and reach the next. If the rope gets stuck two pitches above, though, you'll seriously regret it. You need to make a good judgment call before combining pitches into a single rappel.

Fatter ropes are heavier, bulkier, and harder to deal with when you're climbing. But they have less chance of being cut—a strong selling point. The skinnier your rope is, the less safety margin you have against sharp edges.

Dry Coated

In a rainstorm or on a wet snow or ice climb, a non-coated rope will gain several times its weight in water, so rope companies manufacture some ropes with dry coatings to keep moisture away. Ice climbers, alpinists, and canyoneers prefer dry-coated ropes because a wet rope loses strength and, if it freezes, you end up with a stiff, unusable cable. Unfortunately, most dry coatings scrape off after a few dozen rock pitches. Dry core coatings last somewhat longer. For rappelling only, there's no need to pay extra for a dry rope.

Static Elongation

The amount a rope stretches when loaded with a 176-pound weight is called the static elongation. For rappelling, it's good to have a static rope, or a dynamic rope with low static elongation.

SINGLE ROPE RAPPEL

If a rappel is half a rope length or less, you can rappel on one rope so there's no knot to snag. Set the middle of the rope at the anchors so one end won't be short. If the rope has no middle mark, work your hands along the rope from both ends to find the middle. If no rings exist, be careful not to burn the slings when feeding the rope through. Tie a stopper knot in both rope ends so you can't rappel off the ends of the ropes (see page 29).

DOUBLE ROPE RAPPEL

If the rappel is longer than half a rope, you'll need two ropes to be able to rappel and retrieve the ropes. Pass one rope through the rappel point and tie the ropes together using one of the rappel knots shown below and on the following pages. On multi-pitch rappels, re-check the knots at every rappel station. Especially beware of knots in new, stiff ropes because they tend to untie themselves.

Square Fisherman's Knot

I usually prefer the square fisherman's—a square knot secured with two fisherman's knots—for joining rappel ropes, because it's secure and easy to untie. NEVER use a square knot without the fisherman's backups!

1) Join the ropes with a square knot. Make sure each strand exits the square knot through the same side of the loop it entered, so you get a symmetrical shape.
2) Secure the square knot on both sides with a double fisherman's backup. This step is crucial!
3) Cinch the square knot tight, then cinch the fisherman's backups tight against the square knot.

Square Fisherman's Knot

It's all on the line with your rappel knot. The square fisherman's is secure and easy to untie.

Overhand Knot

The overhand knot is quickest for joining rappel ropes, and it's easy to untie. It's gained widespread acceptance over the past few years, though it still makes me nervous with slick, stiff, or large diameter ropes. Some say it's the best knot for joining rappel ropes, but if this knot makes you nervous, it's not the best knot. The overhand knot does create the smallest profile, so it decreases the chance of getting your ropes stuck. Avoid using the overhand knot on ropes of significantly different diameters, and be careful with stiff, slick, or fat ropes.

1) Grab both ends of the rope, twist them into a coil, and pass the ends out through the coil.
2) Make the tails around ten inches long. Tie a second overhand knot in one of the rope strands to prevent the first knot from slipping.
3) Cinch both knots tight (important!), with the single-strand overhand set snugly against the double-strand overhand.
4) You can also back up the overhand knot with a second, identical knot tied into both rope strands a couple inches from the first knot, but this increases the knot's profile.

The overhand knot has the slimmest profile of the rappel knots, so it's least likely to get jammed. It's not as secure as the other rappel knots, though. The overhand must be tied with a nice long tail, in ropes that aren't too slick or stiff.

Overhand Knot

Double Fisherman's Knot

The double fisherman's is the traditional knot for joining rappel ropes, but it's better for fastening accessory cord (such as perlon, spectra, Titan, Gemini, HT, and Tech cord) into loops than for rigging anchors and slinging chocks. After rappelling, the double fisherman's can be difficult to untie, especially with skinny or wet ropes, so the square fisherman's and overhand knots are better for joining rappel ropes.

1) Coil the free end of one rope twice around the second rope and pass the end out through the coils.
2) Now coil the second rope around the first (in the opposite direction) and pass its end through the coils. The finished knots should be parallel to each other.
3) Pull all four strands coming out of the knots to cinch them tight. The tails should be around three inches long.

The double fisherman's is a traditional rappel knot, but it's hard to untie after being weighted, especially if the rope is wet. It is the best knot for tying cord into loops for slinging chocks.

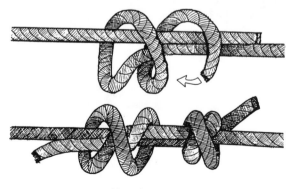

Double Fisherman's Knot

Figure-8 Fisherman's Knot

The figure-8 fisherman's is totally secure, so it's great for joining two topropes or ropes that will be rappelled on multiple times. The large profile of this knot does increase the chance of getting your ropes stuck when you pull it down.

1) Secure the ropes together with a figure-8 knot, leaving both tails fifteen to eighteen inches long. The ends should exit through different sides of the figure-8.
2) Tie a fisherman's backup knot on each side of the figure-8.

The figure-8 fisherman's is the most secure of the rappel knots. Use it when the ropes will be used for multiple rappels or for toproping.

Figure-8 Fisherman's Knot

Stopper Knot

It's important to tie a stopper knot in both ends of the rappel rope(s) before you toss them down, so you can't accidentally rappel off the ends of the rope. This is especially crucial during bad weather, if it's dark, or if you're not very experienced. The stopper knot does increase the chance of getting the rope stuck, especially if the wind is blowing the ropes around or if the rock is textured with rope-snagging features. If you don't use a stopper knot, pay extreme attention to avoid rappelling off the ends of the ropes; far too many climbers have died this way.

A separate overhand or figure-8 knot in each rope end also works as a stopper knot. Some people tie both rope ends together, but this prevents kinks from untwisting at the end of the rope, causing tangled ropes. Untie the stopper knots before pulling your rope or the knot will jam at the rappel point.

1) A stopper knot is similar to the double fisherman's knot. Coil the rope three or four times around itself and pass the end out through the coils.
2) Pull both ends to cinch the knot tight. Make sure the tail is at least three inches long.
3) Tie a second stopper knot in the other end of the rappel rope(s).

Stopper knots in the ends of the ropes can prevent you from rappelling off the ends of the ropes, a measure that has saved many lives.

Stopper Knot

FAT AND SKINNY ROPE

A potential problem exists if you're rappelling on a thick rope tied to a thin one (more than 1.5 millimeters difference), with the thin rope running through the rappel point. When you rappel, the skinny rope can stretch more than the fat one, causing it to slip through the rappel rings. This is especially bad if the rope runs directly through slings because the rope could saw through the slings.

It's better to pass the fat rope through the rappel point and let the knot jam in the rappel rings. This prevents the thin rope from out-stretching the thick one. If the thin rope were cut, you'd still be anchored by the knot jammed in the rings (provided the rings are small enough). Two problems can develop here. When making multi-pitch rappels on two ropes, you usually alternate the rope that passes through the rings because you rig the lower station before pulling the ropes from the higher station. So if you rig so you always pull the skinny rope, you'll lose some efficiency. And if your rope gets stuck with the end out of reach, you'll have only the thin rope for protection while freeing the fat rope.

Rappel Devices

A multitude of rappel devices are available. Some work better than others in certain situations. Often choosing a device is a matter of personal preference. Before we review these devices, let's first briefly consider another essential piece of rappelling gear, the harness.

HARNESSES

The climbing harness connects you to the rope and your anchors. Choose a harness that's comfortable and fits well. The leg loops should allow free leg movement, and the waist belt must be small enough that it cannot pull over your hips. It's helpful if the harness has a belay loop. Use the harness according to manufacturer's instructions, paying special attention to the buckle. Use only harnesses that are in good condition, less than five to eight years old.

RAPPEL DEVICES

Tubes and Plates

Manufacturers offer many styles of tube- and plate-style rappel devices. For climbers, these make excellent belay devices, and they're decent for rappelling. To rappel on a single fixed rope, pass a bight through one of the device's slots and clip it into a locking carabiner on your harness belay loop. If you have two rope strands, pass a bight of each rope through the rappel device slots and clip both strands into the locking carabiner. Visually check to make sure both ropes are clipped.

Most devices have a cable or keeper loop. Keep the loop clipped into the carabiner when rigging or un-rigging the device, so you can never drop it. Tube and plate belay/rappel devices allow the rope to wear out locking carabiners over time. Replace carabiners when the wear becomes noticeable. Most of the tube devices taper so they have a big end and a small end. Usually, you orient the large end toward the carabiner so the rope feeds smoothly for belaying. When rappelling, the small end goes toward the carabiner for maximum friction. If the rope frequently locks up and gives a "jerky" rappel, clip a second carabiner into your harness and the rope to smooth things out.

1. A belay/rappel plate with a spring is smooth and effective, but the spring is a nuisance when you're carrying the device. Pass a bight of each rope through the device's slots and clip the bights into your harness with a locking carabiner. The plate has a keeper cord, so you can't drop it.

2 and 3. A tube device works well for belaying and rappelling. Rig it like a plate device.

4. The Jaws belay/ rappel device has V-shaped grooves that the rope runs through so you can easily vary the friction to meet your needs.

Figure-8

Figure-8s come in many sizes and styles. They're simple to rig, and they give a nice, smooth ride. For sport rappelling a figure-8 is probably the way to go. For climbing I prefer a tube belay/ rappel device—they're better than figure-8s for belaying, plus they're lighter, more compact, and they kink the ropes less when you rappel. Nonetheless, many people prefer figure-8s for rappelling.

One potential problem with figure-8s occurs when the rope rides up over the device, girth hitching the figure-8 and locking up your rappel. You can use this technique for stopping, but to resume rappelling you must unweight the device and remove the girth hitch.

If you're not careful when rappelling with a figure-8, twists in the rope can pass through the figure-8, possibly causing stuck ropes. Clip a sling to your harness and one of the ropes to keep twists from passing up the ropes.

A figure-8 rappel device is easy to rig and gives a smooth rappel, but it's not as good as tubes and plates for belaying. Pass a bight of each rappel rope through the large hole in the figure-8.

Pass the bight around the neck of the figure-8.

Clip the small hole of the figure-8 to your harness and add an autoblock backup (see page 37).

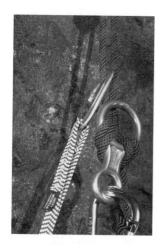

The last person down should clip a sling to one of the ropes. This keeps the ropes from twisting around each other, which could make them difficult or impossible to retrieve from below.

Rappelling with a figure-8 device, an autoblock backup, and a sling clipped to prevent the ropes from twisting.

GriGris

The GriGri is a self-locking belay/rappel device that works well for rappelling a **single line.** Push the cam in to descend. If you let go, it halts your rappel immediately. With a GriGri you can easily stop—no autoblock backup is necessary. A GriGri is the tool of choice among climbing photographers, route setters, riggers, and wall climbers. The bad side is that a GriGri can get so hot when rappelling that it glazes the sheath of your rope, partially melting the nylon. A GriGri must be rigged properly for rappelling. The rope coming from the anchors must go into the slot marked by the little man engraved on the device. The rope going to the brake hand must exit the slot marked by a hand.

Rappelling on two lines with a GriGri is inconvenient, but it's possible. Rig the ropes through the anchors as you normally would. Tie a figure-8 just below the knot joining the ropes and clip it to the second rope with a carabiner, preferably locking. Rappel on the second rope. After you reach the ground or the next rappel stance, pull on the knotted strand to retrieve the rope. Usually you can bring the carabiner down slowly, but if it hits hard against the rock, it may be damaged. Inspect and possibly retire the carabiner if it smashes into the rock or ground.

NOTE: Using GriGris requires special knowledge that does not apply to other belay/rappel devices. Petzl supplies an excellent instructional booklet with all GriGris; please consult this pamphlet before attempting to use a GriGri.

A GriGri works well for rappelling on a single line, and it stops you cold if you let go of it. However, it can get so hot inside that it glazes the sheath of your rope.

The rope must be rigged correctly. The rope exiting the side of the GriGri marked by the little man goes to the anchors. The side marked by the hand goes to the brake hand. Now depress the cam or pull the lever to descend, and let go of the cam or lever to stop.

Carabiners

With five or six carabiners, you can improvise a rappel device in an emergency situation, such as if you drop your regular rappel device. Clip a locking carabiner (or two carabiners with gates opposed) onto your belay loop. Now clip two carabiners onto this one, with gates opposed, to create your "platform" carabiners. (Avoid wire gate carabiners here.) Pass a bight of each rappel line through the platform carabiners. Clip two more carabiners through these bights, then clip them to the rope strands above the carabiners. Slide these two brake carabiners down so they cross the platform carabiners. **The ropes must run across the spines of both brake carabiners—not across the gates.**

1. It's good to know how to fashion a rappel device with just carabiners, in case you lose your device. Clip a locking carabiner to your harness belay loop, then clip two carabiners to it, with gates opposed, to serve as the platform carabiners. Do not use wire gate carabiners for the platform.

2. Pass a bight of each rappel line through the platform carabiners.

3. Clip a carabiner through these bights and onto the strands of rope leading up to the anchors.

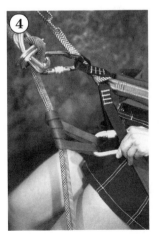

4. Slide the carabiner down over the platform carabiners to serve as a "brake bar." Clip a second carabiner and slide it in next to the first one. Now add an autoblock backup (see page 37).

5. Double-check the entire rigging, and rappel.

1. If you have a large, pear-shaped locking carabiner, you can Munter hitch both rope strands into the carabiner to rappel. Keep the brake side of the rope away from the carabiner gate, or it could unscrew the locking gate.

2. With normal-size carabiners, you can make a Munter hitch in each rope and clip them into separate locking or opposed carabiners. Extend one set of carabiners longer than the other so they don't pinch against each other and lock the ropes. If you look closely you can see why locking or opposed carabiners are important: One of the carabiner gates is being pushed open by a strand of rope. Use this setup as a last resort because the Munter hitches will kink the rope.

Munter Hitch

With a large, pear-shaped locking carabiner (sometimes called an HMS carabiner) clipped to your harness, you can make a Munter hitch in both strands of rope and clip it into the carabiner to rappel. This system is commonly used in Europe. The Munter hitch twists the ropes, so use it as a last resort.

If you don't have a carabiner large enough to accommodate both ropes, you can make a separate Munter hitch in each rope and clip them to different locking carabiners on your harness. Extend one of the Munter hitch carabiners with an extra locking carabiner, or two opposed carabiners, or the ropes will pinch each other and lock up. The rope that goes to your brake hand should exit on the spine side of the carabiner so it's less likely to unscrew the locking carabiner.

To make a Munter hitch:
1) Twist a coil into the rope and fold the upper strand under the lower strand.
2) Clip a locking carabiner into both sides of the folded strand. Orient the Munter hitch with the load strand next to the carabiner's spine.

Munter Hitch

Rappel Racks

Rappel racks are used in caving, rescue, and canyoneering applications. The advantage of a rappel rack is that you can easily adjust the amount of friction. The disadvantage is that they are heavy and bulky to carry. We only briefly mention them here because their use should be accompanied by knowledge and techniques beyond the scope of this book. See a caving or rescue book.

Safety Backups

For safe rappelling, it's important to use backups—a safety double check, an autoblock to back up the brake hand, nuts or cams to back up the fixed anchors, and stopper knots at the rope ends so you can't rappel off the ropes.

DOUBLE CHECK

It's imperative to double-check your systems before committing your life to a rappel. Double-check your harness buckle, anchors, rappel device, autoblock, and the knot joining the ropes. Make sure both ropes are inside your rappel carabiner, that the carabiner is locked, and that the rope runs properly through the rappel point.

AUTOBLOCK

Shortly before his tragic death in an avalanche, Alex Lowe was hit by a rock on Great Trango Tower. He lost control of his rappel and fell all the way to the ends of his ropes before his stopper knots halted him. If he had been using an autoblock backup, he would have stopped immediately after letting go of the ropes.

Currently, most climbers and rappellers in the United States do not use the autoblock backup. It's sort of like parking your car on a steep hill without setting the parking brake—you'll probably be okay, but one day you might return to find your car missing. Only instead of your car, it will be your life. Use the backup.

Backing up the rappel takes a few extra seconds, but it pays off. You can easily stop and use both hands to free twists and tangles, or scout the rappel route. And if you begin accelerating out of control, the friction knot locks automatically and stops your rappel. The backup also adds friction to the rappel, so it's easier to control.

The best rappel backup knot is the autoblock because it's quick to rig and easy to use. Just clip a sling into your leg loop, wrap it several times around the rappel ropes *below* the rappel device, and clip it back to the leg loop. To rappel, hold the autoblock loose in your guide or brake hand. To stop, ease your grip on the autoblock. (A prusik, Klemheist, or other friction knot can be used in place of the autoblock).

Six-millimeter perlon cord works well for the autoblock, but I prefer a 9/16-inch, shoulder-length nylon sling because it's a standard piece of gear with many uses. Nylon webbing creates good friction, while Spectra webbing doesn't grab quite as well. One-inch-wide webbing is too wide to work well.

When you tie the autoblock, keep the sling free of twists and make sure you have the proper number of wraps around the ropes—four or five usually work well. It helps to use up most of

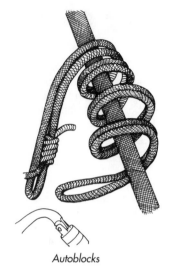
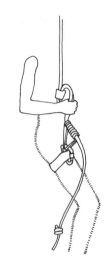

Autoblocks

1. The autoblock should be an essential part of your rappel setup. The autoblock makes it easy to control the rappel and easy to stop, and it could save your life if something causes you to let go of the rope. Clip a ⁹⁄₁₆-inch or so sling, preferably nylon, into your leg loop on the brake hand side.

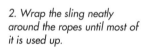
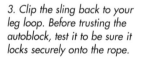

2. Wrap the sling neatly around the ropes until most of it is used up.

3. Clip the sling back to your leg loop. Before trusting the autoblock, test it to be sure it locks securely onto the rope.

4. Look ma', no hands. With the autoblock, you can free your hands to clear rope tangles and arrange the next anchors. If a rock pops you in the noggin, the autoblock will lock up your rappel, possibly saving your life.

To rappel with the autoblock, you need to hold it in your hand to keep it from locking onto the rope. You can hold it with your guide hand and keep the brake hand below;

or you can keep your guide hand above the rappel device and brake hand on the autoblock.

the sling in the wraps. With too many wraps you'll get so much friction that you can barely move. Too few and the autoblock won't engage when you need it, especially if you have a single rope or new, slippery ropes. Test the autoblock to be sure it grabs the rope before trusting it. You may have to experiment to find the right sling and number of wraps for a given rope combination. Keep the sling's stitching or knot outside the autoblock, and retire your sling when it starts to show wear.

Be careful not to let the autoblock get sucked into your rappel device. If you connect the rappel device to your belay loop and rig the autoblock close to your leg loop, this shouldn't be a problem. For harnesses with no belay loop, some climbers girth hitch two slings to the harness tie-in point and rig the rappel device to these.

The autoblock adds friction so you don't burn your hands on steep rappels. If you let go of the rope, the autoblock locks up. When locked, the autoblock never holds full body weight, just the amount held by your brake hand, so it's easy to loosen to resume rappelling. If you do start to lose control of the rappel, let go of the autoblock (or other friction backup knot) so it can grip the rope. Several have died because they kept a grip on the backup, and it never locked onto the rope.

The old-school technique of rigging a prusik knot (or other friction knot) above the belay device and clipping it to your belay loop still works for backing up the rappel. This system is better if

you have to rappel past a knot or if something gets jammed in your rappel device, but still, the autoblock system is easier to use and safer in most situations. If you do rig a prusik above the rappel device, hold the prusik in your guide (top) hand when rappelling. Make sure the prusik is clipped close enough to your harness that it cannot escape your reach, possibly stranding you on a steep rappel. At least one rappeller has perished this way.

A mechanical device called the Petzl Shunt has a "deadman" lever—let go and it locks up your rappel. It makes a great rappel backup, if you don't mind carrying it. The Petzl Shunt is highly recommended for sport rappelling and spelunking.

A prusik tied above the rappel device is the old-school rappel backup. It can still work, but don't tie it off too long, like this rappeller did. Now it's locked onto the rope, out of her reach, and she might be stranded.

STOPPER KNOTS

The stopper knots discussed earlier are a crucial part of your backup system. Stopper knots prevent the possibility of rappelling off the ends of your ropes, a horrible ending that has surprised too many rappellers. For stopper knots to work with a figure-8 device, you need an autoblock backup set below the figure-8. Otherwise, the stopper knots will go whizzing through the figure-8.

Mark Wilford was once retreating in a winter storm on the Grey Pillar of Longs Peak. His heavy pack pulled him out of control, and he whipped down the ropes. Just before he flew off the ends of the ropes and down the wall, they flipped around and twisted—and amazingly, stopped him. Now Mark ties the ropes together at the bottom and clips a sling from his harness to one of the ropes to prevent going off the ends. This does cause the ropes to occasionally twist up, but it's better than no backup at all.

ANCHOR BACKUP

Unless your rappel anchors are absolutely bombproof, it's good to have one or two backup anchors as described in the anchor chapter. When the first person arrives at the station, he or she sets the backups and clips into the fixed anchors and the backups. The backups give extra protection to the party until the last person removes them and rappels. The backups should not bear weight so the fixed anchors get tested. If the fixed anchors are really bad, the backups should be left in place.

FIREMAN'S BELAY

If you hold the ropes from below as your partner rappels, you can pull the ropes tight and halt his rappel if he loses control. This is a great way to belay an inexperienced partner after you've already rappelled—provided you can see them for the entire rappel. If both rappellers are experienced and using autoblock backups, though, there's no real need for a fireman's belay.

PADDING THE ROPE FROM SHARP EDGES

When possible, it's important to pad the ropes from sharp edges. This is more practical and critical when rappelling fixed ropes. Pad the dangerous edge with a shirt, pack, specially designed rope pad, or duct tape before rappelling below it.

HELMET

Falling rocks constitute one of the greatest hazards faced by climbers and rappellers. While a helmet cannot protect you from huge rocks, it can save your life if a smaller rock hits you in the head or if your head strikes the rock in a fall. Buy a good climbing helmet and wear it whenever you climb or rappel.

Use a pack, shirt, sleeping pad, or duct tape to pad sharp rock edges. This is most practical when you're rappelling a fixed rope.

"On Rappel!"

Now that you've got the anchors, equipment, and safety backups down, it's time to rappel. The complexity of rappelling increases drastically with a multi-pitch descent. For efficiency when climbing and rappelling long routes, all partners should keep busy—always be thinking, "What can I do right now to speed us up?"

RIGGING THE RAPPEL

Make sure everyone is safely clipped into the rappel anchors while rigging the rappel. Set the ropes through the rappel point, tie them together, yell, **"Rope!,"** and throw them down. Or, if you're rappelling a single line, tie one end into the anchors and toss the rope. Now the first rappeller rigs his rappel device onto the rope(s), adds an autoblock backup, double-checks the rigging, and prepares to rappel. It's helpful to hold the rope while your partner rigs her rappel so she doesn't have to battle the weight of the rope.

Getting Started

The classic rappel position: feet shoulder-width apart, knees slightly bent, legs almost perpendicular to the wall, torso upright, guide hand on the autoblock, and brake hand just below.

Every rappeller should know the prime rule of rappelling: **Never let go of the rope with your brake hand.** (With a properly rigged autoblock, you actually can let go, after ensuring that the autoblock is locked firmly onto the rope.) Your other hand, the guide hand, should lightly hold the rope above your belay device for balance, or it can grasp the autoblock backup with the brake hand below, which gives you two brake hands. Some rappellers wear a leather glove on the brake hand or on both hands. This can be helpful, but it's unnecessary when using an autoblock.

Before starting the rappel, yell, **"On Rappel!"** if there's a chance anybody is below you. They should get out of the way to avoid any rocks you might accidentally kick loose.

If you're starting from a cliff top, let the rappel device take your weight and slowly walk back toward the edge. Leaning back on the rappel line is counter-intuitive and can be terrifying the first time you do it. It gets easier with experience, but it's good to always keep a healthy fear and respect for rappelling.

At the lip, plant your feet and lower your butt until you're in the classic rappel position—legs nearly perpendicular to the rock, knees slightly bent, feet shoulder-width apart, and body

(opposite page) Descending from Bridger Jack Butte near Canyonlands National Park, Utah.

Keep hair and shirt tails away from your rappel device. This rappeller is in a bad situation.

bent at the waist so your torso is upright. Stay leaned back so your feet push into the wall. If you get too far upright, your feet will slip and you'll eat the rock. It doesn't taste good, believe me.

If you're beginning your rappel from a small ledge, or no ledge at all, it's easier to start. Just weight the rope (being careful not to put an outward pull on the anchors) and go.

Let the rope pass through the rappel device as you "walk" backward down the rock face. Walk smoothly down the face—a bouncy or jerky rappel places extra stress on the anchors. A slow rappel is safer than leaping and bounding down the face because it's easier to maintain control.

Keep clothing and long hair tucked in while rappelling—it can be painful and even dangerous if it gets jammed in your rappel device. If something ever does get jammed in your rappel device, you need to unweight the device, if possible. You'd be happy to have an autoblock backup so you could use both hands to free yourself. You might need to set a second friction knot on the rope above your rappel device, clip a sling to it, and stand up in the sling to truly unweight the rappel device.

One guy got his shirt stuck in his rappel device and tried to cut himself free with a knife. His knife touched one of the taut ropes, and he came free in a hurry—after the rope cut.

If you ever knock a rock loose or see a rock falling, yell, **"ROCK!"** to alert anyone below—often your partner who's rappelled before you. Yell the same thing—**"ROCK!"**—if you drop a piece of gear because any falling object represents a danger to people below. Yell, **"ROCK!"** regardless of whether you think people are below or not. People have been killed by rockfall let loose by people above who were certain nobody was below.

*(opposite page)
Watch out for loose rocks and rocks falling from above. One of the most dangerous times is when you pull your rappel ropes down. Be alert while pulling the ropes and for a few seconds after the ropes come down.*

If rocks are falling toward you and you can't escape them, tuck into the wall as tight as you can, under an overhang, if possible. If you don't have a helmet, bad choice; now you can only cover your head with your hands. If you do have a helmet, don't cover your head with your hands—one guy lost a finger that way.

More Friction

A standard rappel device with a properly rigged autoblock backup should give plenty of friction. Some rappellers forgo the autoblock. In that case, if it's steep and you're rappelling on one rope, new ropes, or skinny ropes, you might want more friction. Clip the rope through a carabiner on your leg loop, or wrap the rope behind your back to gain friction. Still, the autoblock is the best way to get extra friction.

1. If you're not using an autoblock, you can get extra friction by passing the brake side of the rope through a carabiner clipped to your leg loop. Bend the rope around this carabiner to gain friction.

2. You can also gain friction by passing the rope behind your back or under your leg. Let the rope run across your harness leg loop if the rope is uncomfortable.

Passing a Roof

To rappel past a roof, set your feet at the lip of the roof, shoulder-width apart. Keep your feet at the lip and lower your body below the roof, until you're sure your body and head will clear the lip. Then, kick your feet free and swing under the roof.

Stopping

Sometimes you want to stop on rappel to clear rope snags, scope the route, or even take a picture. With an autoblock backup, you can easily lock the rope to stop and have both hands free. You can also wrap the ropes around one of your legs four or five times to stop a rappel and free your hands. However, this is less convenient and less secure.

A mule knot can be used to tie off your rappel device securely, and it can be easily untied when weighted. Be sure your brake hand is ready to take the weight when you untie the mule.

If you have an autoblock, it's easy to stop as shown earlier. If not, you can stop by wrapping the ropes several times around your leg. This may not be comfortable if you're wearing shorts.

To tie the mule:
1) Pass a bight of rope near your brake hand through the rappel carabiner (two bights if you're rappelling on two ropes).
2) Twist a coil into the rope(s) that you passed through the carabiner, then pass a loop around the load strand and back through the coil to create a "slip" knot.
3) Secure the mule knot with an overhand or fisherman's knot.

You can also tie the rope off securely to your rappel device with a load-releasable mule knot. This would be unnecessary if you were using the autoblock, but it is a very secure tie-off.

Mule Knot

First One Down

The first rappeller down has several duties.
1) Clear all rope tangles and snags on the way down. Always clear snags before you rappel below them. You might be unable to free them from below, and you could pull a rock down on yourself trying.
2) Keep the rope(s) away from sharp edges.
3) Watch out for loose rocks.
4) Look for the next rappel station.
5) Be super aware of the rope ends so you can't rappel off of them. They should be fixed with stopper knots to avoid this possibility.
6) Inspect the anchors at the next station.
7) Reinforce the anchors if they're not bomber and rearrange the rigging if it's messy.

8) Clip yourself into the anchors and double-check the clip-in.
9) Clip the rappel lines into the anchors if the rappel above was diagonal or overhanging.
10) Dismantle your rappel device from the rope(s).
11) Yell, **"Off Rappel!"** to inform your partner that the rope is free.
12) Feed the rope to be pulled through the next rappel links as your partner descends, and tie a new stopper knot in the ends of the rope.
13) Give a fireman's belay to your partner if he's not very experienced.

Last One Down

The last person down has fewer duties, but they are important.
1) Make sure the ropes remain untwisted above so they pull easily.
2) Keep the ropes free from cracks or other constrictions that might jam them. Rappel down the "cleanest" section of the face possible.
3) Be careful not to knock loose rocks down on your partners below, and yell, **"Rock!"** if you do see any falling rocks.

Never rappel below a snag in the rope. You may not be able to free it from below, or you could pull a rock down on yourself trying. Free snags before you rappel below them.

Route Finding

The first rappeller is in charge of finding the way down. This is usually pretty easy—just rappel from station to station. Occasionally, though, a station can be tricky to find. If you're rappelling the route you climbed, you already have knowledge about where to go. If not, watch carefully for the next station while you rappel.

A topographic map of the route can be helpful. Make the rappels long if you're retreating on your own gear, unless the rock has lots of rope-snagging features. Be careful not to rappel below the last anchor possibilities, though. The first one down should know how to ascend the rope and have the equipment to do so, in case he reaches the end of the ropes with no good anchor possibilities in sight or rappels past a roof and can't get back into the rock.

Tossing the Ropes

To toss the ropes down in preparation for the next rappel, lower the upper ten to thirty feet of rope. Stack the upper half of what's left of the rope back and forth across your hand and toss it, while holding the middle of the rope. Now stack the free end. Yell, **"Rope!"** and throw it out hard, trying to clear all obstacles.

Toss the second rope the same way. It's often hard to toss ropes all the way down, so the first rappeller may have to untangle and re-toss the ropes as he descends.

Avoid tossing your ropes into the trees on the final rappel to the ground. If a party is below, it's much more polite to lower your ropes down slowly, with the bottom end coming first.

In extremely high winds, you may want to rappel with the ropes stacked in a sling, rope bag, or pack, so you can feed them out as you go. Tie them in when you reach the next station. This prevents the ropes from blowing around the side of the mountain and getting stuck. When pulling the ropes down in high winds, give them a hard downward tug the instant they start to fall, and duck.

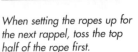

When setting the ropes up for the next rappel, toss the top half of the rope first.

Then toss the end of the rope out from the rock to clear any rope-snagging features.

Pulling the Ropes

Remove the stopper knots and tangles from the rope before pulling it down. Once you start pulling, keep the rope moving so it won't lodge in a constriction. While one rappeller pulls the rope down, the other feeds it through the next rappel anchors (unless they're on the ground). In that case, walking away from the cliff reduces the bend of the rope if it runs around a ledge, making an easier pull.

An instant before the rope starts to fall, whip it hard outward. This makes the rope fly away from the cliff and helps prevent stuck ropes. Keep your eyes and ears peeled for loose rocks knocked down by the ropes. Helmets give good protection against small, loose rocks.

A falling rope can snap you like a bullwhip if you don't get out of the way. Once at Devils Tower, our falling rappel line popped the ground so hard that four inches of the rope frayed. Imagine catching that in your teeth. Always yell, **"Rope!"** as it starts to

If the rope is hard to pull down, two people can work together to pull it.

To help the rope clear rope-sticking obstacles, whip it out away from the rock just before the free end falls through the anchors.

fall, and take cover. Far too often I've had rappel ropes dropped on my head by another party without warning, which is really lame and potentially dangerous.

After the rope falls down, pull the free end up and tie a stopper knot. Yell, **"Rope!"** again and toss it down for the next rappel. Both climbers must be careful to never drop the ropes. Always have them tied in or fed through rappel rings or links. On the Rupal Face of Nanga Parbat—the world's tallest mountain face—Barry Blanchard and Kevin Doyle dropped their rappel ropes during an epic retreat. They both assumed the other was taking care of the ropes. You probably won't be as lucky—they miraculously stumbled across a cache of ropes left by a Japanese expedition.

Hanging Rappel Transfer

An exciting situation in rappelling is the hanging rappel transfer. It's like any other multi-pitch rappel, except that no ledge exists and you hang full body weight on the anchors. Like always, it's helpful to have a cow's tail or daisy chain girth hitched to your harness for clipping the anchors. Always clip into an equalized point of the anchors, or at least be clipped to all of the anchors. Be extra careful, double- and triple-checking every step to make sure you've got it right!

Here we have two rappellers clipped into a two-bolt anchor station. Both rappellers are clipped into each of the bolts with cow's tails (see page 13). One rappeller holds the weight of the rope to make it easier for the other to rig her rappel device.

After rigging the rappel device and autoblock backup, both rappellers double-check the rappel setup.

The first rappeller heads down to the next anchor station. On the way she must free any rope snags.

After finding and inspecting the soundness of the anchors, she clips into them.

Now she begins feeding the rope for the next rappel, while her partner rigs his rappel above. He can set the autoblock while she's rappelling. When she's finished and has unweighted the rope, he pulls some slack through the autoblock and rigs his rappel device.

After double-checking his own setup, the second rappeller heads down to the next station.

He clips in, double-checks, and dismantles his rappel setup.

She pulls down the rope, while he feeds it through the rings for the next rappel.

They set the knot joining the ropes at the rappel point. It's important to watch that the free end of the rope has no twists or knots that would jam it above. They finish pulling the ropes and rig them for the next rappel.

She rigs for the next rappel,

they double-check everything again, and

she rappels. They repeat this process all the way to the ground.

A jammed rope can be impossible to pull down.

Stuck Ropes

Seven hundred feet up a thousand foot wall, black clouds pour over the skyline. A few drops of rain give scant warning, then the deluge hits. In minutes you're soaked to the bone, the wind is whipping, and the rock is Teflon-slick. Time to go down.

After the leader abandons some protection anchors and lowers back to the belay, your team switches from climbing to rappelling. Imagine that two rappels down, with three more to go, the rope gets stuck above. You try whipping it out from the rock to clear the jam. You pull harder and harder, but it won't budge. A frigid wind is cranking, you're becoming chilled, and darkness is two hours away. What are you going to do?

The best way to deal with stuck ropes is to avoid getting them stuck in the first place. Avoiding stuck ropes is part experience, part foresight, and part luck. On a steep, smooth rock face, ropes usually pull nicely. If the angle is low, the rock is highly featured, or if the rope runs over an abrupt edge or through a crack, the chance of sticking a rope increases.

To avoid stuck ropes, survey the terrain for cracks, vegetation, flakes, or other features that can snag the rope. The last person down keeps the rope free from these obstacles and makes sure no twists pass up the rope. If you have two rappel lines, always note which rope to pull from below before you rappel, and tell your partner. If you pull on the wrong rope, the knot won't pull through the anchors. Worse, the rope could get stuck.

When pulling the rope, once it starts moving, keep it moving. Make sure no twists or knots exist in the free end. At the end of the pull, just before the rope falls through the top anchors, whip it hard outward, away from the cliff, to help it fly past rope-snagging obstacles. Don't do this in forested terrain or you may snag your rope in the trees. Even if you do everything right, the ropes can still get stuck. I once had to re-climb a pitch to free a rope. The rope had tied an overhand knot in itself and jammed just before it flipped through the anchors.

If you anticipate problems with the rope pulling, the first climber down should test pull it for a few feet before the last person rappels, then reset it to the middle. This can also be the "off rappel" signal in high winds or in a canyon with a loud river. If the rope won't pull, the last rappeller may have to: (1) run the rope through rappel rings or carabiners rather than the nylon slings; (2) extend the rappel point with webbing; or (3) set the knot joining the rappel ropes below the rappel ledge. In the third example, the last rappeller must downclimb or hand-over-hand down the rope to get below the knot and begin rappelling. The last rappeller should definitely have an autoblock backup.

If the whole team is at the lower rappel station and the rope won't pull, try pulling or flipping the rope out of a crack or other snag. If you're on the ground, walk out from the base of the cliff to change the pulling angle. If those tricks don't work, tug harder to see if you can get it moving. Be careful, though—if the rope is stuck in a crack, pulling too hard can jam it permanently. It's important to carry a knife in case your rope does become hopelessly stuck in a crack, so you can cut it free and use what's left to get down. If the rope just won't pull, you may have to climb the rock or the rope to solve the problem.

ASCENDING A STUCK ROPE

If you have mechanical ascenders, consider yourself lucky. Anchor one of the ropes and climb the other rope with the ascenders. Once you're at the anchors, fix the problem that caused the stuck rope and rappel again.

Lacking mechanical ascenders? An improvised rope ascent may be your salvation. Climbing the rope could also save the day if you accidentally rappel past an overhang and have no way to reach anchors, if you rappel down the wrong route and no anchors exist, or if you mistakenly pass the anchors and have to climb back up to them. Rigging to climb a rope quickly and efficiently takes practice—don't wait until you're stranded in a rainstorm to learn!

With two friction knots—knots that lock onto the rope when weighted, but can be slid up the rope when unweighted—you can easily climb the rope. Simply slide one friction knot up, weight it, slide the other friction knot up, transfer your weight onto it, then slide the first one up again.

The best friction knot for rope ascending is the Bachman because it slides up the easiest. Weight the sling to lock the Bachman—if you weight the carabiner it will slip. Avoid carabiners with a "scalloped" spine—they may not provide enough friction. If the Bachman slips when weighted, try re-wrapping it, or substitute thinner webbing or cord, or use a prusik knot instead. The prusik gives more friction, but it's harder to slide up the rope. A Klemheist will also work for climbing the rope.

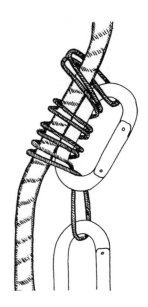

To rig a Bachman:
1) Clip a carabiner into a sling or loop of cord.
2) Wrap the sling or cord three to five times around the rope and through the carabiner, keeping the wraps free of twists.
3) Weight the loop exiting the carabiner. If the Bachman slips when weighted, add more wraps.

Bachman

If you have to climb a stuck rope, life is much easier if you have ascenders. Provided that the ropes still run through the rappel anchors, and that you still have both ropes, tie one rope off to the anchors. Climb the other rope with the ascenders. Make sure both ascenders are clipped to your harness with locking carabiners and that each one has a foot loop. Also tie a backup knot in the rope you'll be climbing and clip it to your harness. Periodically re-tie a new backup knot, clip it, then unclip the old one and untie it.

Slide both ascenders as high as possible to start. Stand up in the foot loop of the lower ascender and slide the higher one up as far as possible. Sit back into the sling or daisy chain attached to your harness, which should be adjusted so it goes tight on your harness when the ascender is almost at full reach. Slide the lower ascender up, stand up, and slide the higher one up again. Sit into it and repeat until you've reached the anchors and can solve the problem that caused the stuck rope.

To tie a prusik:

1) Tie a piece of cord (5 or 6 millimeters in diameter) into a loop with a double fisherman's knot.
2) Girth hitch the loop around the rope to be ascended.
3) Pass the loop back through the center of the girth hitch one to three more times. Dress the prusik cleanly (without twists) to ensure maximal bite on the climbing rope.
4) Load the loop coming out of the prusik to see if it "bites." If the prusik slips, add more wraps or try a smaller diameter cord.

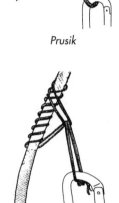

Prusik

To make a Klemheist:

1) Wrap a loop of cord or a webbing sling four or five revolutions up the rope.
2) Pass the other end of the sling through the final loop and clip into the sling where it exits the loop.
3) Add more wraps if the Klemheist slips, and keep the wraps tidy.

Some climbers and rappellers carry two pieces of perlon pre-tied to the correct lengths for creating friction knots. It's not a bad idea, but you'll rarely need these special perlon loops. For overall efficiency it's more sensible to ascend the rope with standard gear like webbing slings or a cordelette. The best thing to use is 9/16-inch and 5/8-inch webbing or 5- to 6-millimeter perlon or Spectra cord. Nylon grips better than Spectra and has a higher melting temperature, so it's the better choice for friction knots, though Spectra slings also work. With cord, the thinner and more supple it is, the better it works for friction knots. Spectra cord is sheathed in nylon, so it works fine for friction knots.

Klemheist

If you're ascending a stuck rappel line, hopefully you have both strands to ascend, with the rope still through the top anchors. In this case, wrap the friction knot around both rope strands.

Climb the Ropes

When practicing rope ascending, it's easiest to start out on a vertical wall. After you've mastered that, try a free-hanging rope, which is more difficult. Practice with a separate toprope and belayer while you work out the system.

1. Lacking ascenders, you'll have to improvise the rope ascent. If you have two shoulder-length slings or one double-length sling, a cordelette, and some locking and non-locking carabiners, you're in business. If you're not on the ground, stay clipped into your anchors until you have the ascending system and backup knots completely set up.

Tie a Bachman knot onto the ropes with a sling. Girth hitch another sling to this one and clip it to your harness belay loop or tie-in point with a locking carabiner. Adjust the sling's length so you can reach two to six inches past the Bachman when hanging on the sling. You can shorten the sling by tying overhand or figure-8 knots in it.

Tie a figure-8 loop in the middle of the cordelette and fix it to the rope(s) with a second Bachman knot, below the sling. Slide both Bachman knots as high as you can. Tie a figure-8 loop in one strand of the cordelette and clip it to your harness, in the same carabiner as the sling. Lock the carabiner. Now tie a foot loop in the other strand of the cordelette, long enough so you can comfortably high step onto it. Some people use both feet in the loop, but one works best for most.

Back up the Bachman knots so you can't crater if they fail. Tie a figure-8 knot in the rope(s) you're about to climb and clip it to your harness with a locking biner (or two carabiners, gates opposed). If you're ascending two ropes, the figure-8 backup should be tied in both strands. If you're starting from flat ground, like this climber, wait until you get up ten feet before tying the backup.

Double-check everything, then unclip (if you're tied into an anchor station).

2. To climb the rope, grab it and stand up in the foot loop. Quickly slide the upper Bachman knot as high as you can reach.

3. Sit into your harness on the Bachman knot and relax. Slide the lower Bachman up until it almost touches the higher one. Stand up in the foot loop, quickly slide the higher Bachman up as high as possible, sit into it, and relax again. Repeat the above process to climb up the rope and free the snag.

Every fifteen to twenty feet, considering the ground and ledges, tie a new backup knot in the rope(s), clip it, then unclip and untie the old one.

Option: Four shoulder-length slings can substitute for the cordelette. One makes the Bachman knot, one connects the Bachman sling to your harness, and two girth hitched together make a foot loop.

4. You can use a prusik instead of a Bachman knot for ascending ropes, but it's harder to slide up after being weighted so it can be slow, strenuous, and aggravating.

One time at Indian Creek, Utah, our rappel line got stuck, with the free end one hundred feet up. I drew the shortest straw and had to jumar the jammed rope—with my weight held by whatever the rope was stuck on. I used the length of rope that we had pulled down, along with occasional protection in the crack, for a belay. It was creepy knowing that the rope could come free at any moment. My "anchor" turned out to be a simple twist of rope jammed in the crack.

Far worse would be having a rope stuck with one end out of reach, many pitches up in a remote location, on a rock face that offered no opportunities for protection. You would have two choices—cut the rope and continue down with what's left of it, or climb the rope trusting your life to the rope jam. Pray it never happens to you.

See *Self Rescue* or *Advanced Rock Climbing,* also in the How to Rock Climb series, for more improvised rope climbing techniques.

Special Situations

OVERHANGING OR DIAGONAL RAPPELS

When rappelling a steeply overhanging wall or a wildly diagonal line where you can't reach the rappel station by rappelling straight down, the first rappeller must clip the ropes back into bolts or cams and nuts along the way to reach the next rappel station. At the next station, he clips himself *and* the ropes in—he must not let the ropes go. The last rappeller down unclips and retrieves the gear left by the first rappeller. When she is slightly below the level of the rappel station, the first climber pulls her in.

RAPPELLING WITH A HEAVY LOAD

If you have a heavy pack or haul bag to carry down the rappels, attach a sling to at least two attachment points on the pack or haulbag. Clip the sling into the belay/rappel loop of your harness with a locking carabiner. Straddle the pack as it hangs from your belay loop. Now it won't pull you over backward while you rappel. The steeper the rappel or the heavier the bag, the more essential this becomes.

RAPPELLING FIXED LINES

When rappelling fixed ropes, you'll usually have only one strand of rope to descend. Be extra careful that the autoblock bites well—the decreased friction of a single rope strand makes it more likely to slip.

If you have to rappel with a heavy pack or haul bag, it's easiest to carry the weight clipped to the belay loop on your harness.

PASSING A KNOT

By passing a knot, you can make a super-long, single-strand rappel on two or more ropes tied together. You might do this when fixing ropes on a wall climb, or to make an emergency evacuation. By passing knots, you can also rappel down a rock-damaged rope, with loops tied to isolate the damaged sections of rope.

With Mechanical Ascenders

If you're on a single strand of rope, a mechanical ascender can make passing a knot easy.

1) Tie a knot in the bottom end of the rope so there's no way you can rappel off it. Rig your rappel device and autoblock on the rope.
2) Rappel until the knot is 1 ½ feet below your rappel device. Lock up the autoblock to stop.
3) Set a mechanical ascender on the rope above your rappel device and clip it to your harness with a sling. Slide the ascender up the rope until the sling goes tight.
4) Let rope pass through the autoblock to transfer your weight onto the ascender.
5) Tie a figure-8 knot three feet below the knot for a backup, and clip it into a tie-in point or belay loop on your harness with a locking carabiner.
6) Dismantle the rappel device and autoblock and re-set them just below the knot. Double-check everything.
7) Attach foot slings to the ascender. Stand in the slings, unclip your harness from the ascender, and climb down the slings until your weight is held by the rappel device and autoblock.
8) Retrieve the ascender and re-check your setup.
9) Untie the figure-8 backup and rappel.

With a Cordelette

A cordelette works for passing knots on one rope strand or two. See photos.

To tie a Munter mule:
1) Rig a Munter hitch onto a locking carabiner.
2) Create a mule knot as described on page 47 by twisting a coil into the non-load strand, then passing a loop around the load strand and back through the coil to create a "slip" knot. Tie the mule knot close to the Munter hitch.
3) Back up the mule with an overhand or a fisherman's knot.

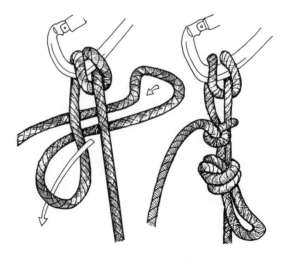

Munter Mule

1. Before rappelling, make a loop in the end of a cordelette and tie it onto the rappel ropes with a Klemheist. Now tie the cordelette to a locking carabiner on your harness with a load-releasable Munter mule knot, so the Klemheist rides a foot above your rappel device. This will substitute for the autoblock as the rappel backup. Double-check the rigging, then rappel, holding the Klemheist with your guide hand.

2. When the knot is 1½ feet below your rappel device, let the Klemheist lock onto the rope.

3. If you have a second rappel device, rig it below the knot and add an autoblock backup. If you don't have a second device, you can substitute a Munter hitch on a locking carabiner.

A third option is to tie a figure-8 knot three feet below the knot and clip it into your harness to back up the cordelette. Remove your rappel device from the rope and re-rig it with an autoblock just below the knot.

4. Double-check everything. Untie the mule knot from the cordelette and lower yourself on the cordelette's Munter hitch until your weight transfers onto the rappel device and autoblock.

5. Retrieve the cordelette, re-check the rigging, and continue rappelling.

If you're with an inexperienced rappeller, you should let your partner rappel first while you belay him from above with a second rope. On multi-pitch descents, though, you shouldn't trust him to locate and clip into the next anchors. The best method here is to pre-rig your partner's rappel device and autoblock. You rappel first and give your partner a fireman's belay from below when he rappels.

To pre-rig an inexperienced partner, girth hitch two *good* slings to his harness tie-in point to form a double "cow's tail." Connect his rappel device to the rope and both girth-hitched slings with a locking carabiner before you rappel. Double-check both your partner's and your own setups before you go. Now, as you rappel and pull the rope tight, the cow's tail extension keeps your partner from getting sucked into the rope. Once you've prepared the next anchors, he's pre-rigged and ready to rappel down to you. Explain how to avoid running the rope across the cow's tail slings as he rappels, and to keep the rope free of any obstacles that might stick it. Point out the specific obstacles that you notice on your way down.

Pre-rigging an inexperienced partner allows you to check her rigging and rappel first to establish the next station. Girth hitch two slings to your partner's harness to create a cow's tail. Rig her rappel device on the ropes, extended with the cow's tail. If you can see her the whole time she rappels, you can give her a fireman's belay. Pull tight on the ropes to stop her descent if she loses control of the rappel. If you can't see her the whole time, she should have an autoblock rappel backup.

SPIDER RAPPEL WITH AN INJURED CLIMBER

The spider rappel allows a rescuer to rappel with an injured climber on a single rappel device. This system also works for guides rappelling with novices.

1) Rig a rappel device on the rope(s) and add an autoblock backup clipped to your leg loop.
2) Tie off a cordelette as shown, with three double-stranded figure-8 knots and one tail longer than the other. The middle figure-8 clips into the rappel device. You can also rig this with slings—double the slings to both rappellers.
3) Clip the short tail to your harness and the long tail to the injured climber's harness, with locking carabiners. This way you hang at different levels so you don't crowd each other. Also, clip the injured party on the side opposite your brake hand.
4) Double-check the rigging and locking carabiners, and test that the autoblock grabs the rope. Now you're ready to go. You control the rappel for yourself and the injured climber. Don't let the rappel rope(s) run across the cordelette or slings connecting you to the rappel device.

The cordelette has been doubled and tied with three figure-8 loops. You can also rig a similar arrangement with nylon slings.

The middle loop goes to the rappel device. The short strand goes to the guide or rescuer, and the long strand goes to the client or injured person.

Adding an autoblock to the system (below her right hand) is essential. Now the rescuer or guide can control the rappel for both rappellers. Even this guide had no trouble controlling the weight of herself and her client who outweighs her by 50 pounds.

SIMUL-RAPPEL

A super-dangerous technique where both climbers rappel simultaneously has been gaining popularity recently. **We totally discourage such simul-rappelling.** It's a deadly proposition for both rappellers if you don't perform every step perfectly; and if another party sees you simul-rappelling, they may do it, too, without understanding the essential backups.

Simul-rappelling doubles the load on your anchors, so they must be completely bomber. Tie stopper knots in both rope ends before tossing them. It's best if the rope runs through relatively small chain links or rappel rings so the knot joining the ropes cannot pass through. Avoid the overhand rappel knot in this case. Triple grapevine backups can fatten the rappel knot a little so it cannot pass through the rappel rings.

The most experienced climber rappels on the rope running through the rings. His weight is held by the knot jammed in the rings, so he's not dependent on the counterweight of his partner. Ideally, he uses a GriGri to rappel. If not, he *must* use an autoblock backup. His partner rigs to rappel on the other rope, also with an autoblock. Her rope depends on his counterweight—if he slacks the rope, she slips down. If he prematurely unclips from the rope, she drops. To back up both rappellers, they tie themselves together with slings or cordelettes, three to five feet apart.

The team now double-checks all the rigging and both harness buckles, and rappels down side by side. Both rappellers avoid running the rappel lines across their slings or belay loops. At the next set of anchors, they clip in, retrieve their rappel line, rig the next rappel, and carry on.

It is extremely dangerous to shortcut the backups. If you forget the stopper knots and your partner rappels off a rope end, he's gone, then you lose your counterweight and you're gone, too. If you forget to tie yourself to your partner with slings or cordelette, and you get down first and instinctively remove the rappel device or lose control, your partner plummets. If one of you orients the GriGri upside-down, both fall. Simul-rappelling also doubles the weight on your anchors and ropes, increasing the chances of anchor failure or cut ropes. The many hazards and double jeopardy of simul-rappelling make it hard to recommend. In fact, this technique has resulted in several fatalities and near fatalities. However, for experienced climbers beating a hasty retreat, the increased speed advantage may outweigh the risks.

CONCLUSION

As in all aspects of climbing, heed the safety rules, be conservative, and double-check all systems before relying on them. By taking great care, you're likely to make it down from all your vertical adventures.

Index

Page numbers in *italics* indicate illustrations or tables.

tossing ropes, 48–49
timely, 12
Titan, 28
topographic map, 48
tossing ropes, 48–49
transfer, hanging rappel, 50–53
trees, 9
Triangle, American, 19
tubes, 31
twin ropes, 25

U

Union Internationale des Associations d'Alpinisme, 25

W

webbing, 37
wire gate carabiners, 35

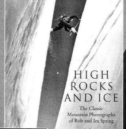

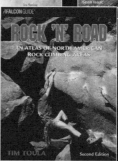

HOW TO CLIMB!

The *How to Climb*™ series includes the top instructional books on rock climbing technique.

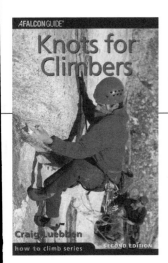

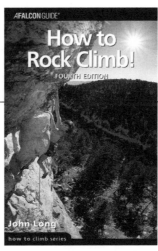

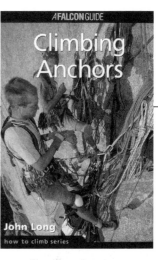

KNOTS FOR CLIMBERS, 2ND
Craig Luebben

HOW TO ROCK CLIMB, 4TH
John Long

CLIMBING ANCHORS
John Long

ADVANCED ROCK CLIMBING
John Long & Craig Luebben

ETTER BOULDERING
John Sherman

BIG WALLS
John Long & John Middendorf

BUILDING YOUR OWN INDOOR CLIMBING WALL
Ramsay Thomas

CLIMB ON! SKILLS FOR MORE EFFICIENT CLIMBING
Hans Florine & Bill Wright

CLIP & GO
John Long & Duane Raleigh

COACHING CLIMBING
Michelle Hurni

GYM CLIMB
John Long

HOW TO ICE CLIMB!
Craig Luebben

HOW TO CLIMB 5.12, 2ND
Eric J. Hörst

RAPPELING
Scott Luebben

MORE CLIMBING ANCHORS
John Long & Bob Gaines

SELF-RESCUE
David Fasulo

SPORT CLIMBING, 3RD
John Long

TOPROPING
S. Peter Lewis

TRAINING FOR CLIMBING
Eric J. Hörst

ACCESS: It's every climber's concern

The Access Fund, a national, non-profit climbers' organization, works to keep climbing areas open and to conserve the climbing environment. Need help with closures? land acquisition? legal or land management issues? funding for trails and other projects? starting a local climbers' group? CALL US!

Climbers can help preserve access by being committed to leaving the environment in its natural state. Here are some simple guidelines:

• **STRIVE FOR ZERO IMPACT** especially in environmentally sensitive areas like caves. Chalk can be a significant impact on dark and porous rock—don't use it around historic rock art. Pick up litter, and leave trees and plants intact.

• **DISPOSE OF HUMAN WASTE PROPERLY** Use toilets whenever possible. If toilets are not available, dig a "cat hole" at least six inches deep and 200 feet from any water, trails, campsites, or the base of climbs. *Always pack out toilet paper.* On big wall routes, use a "poop tube" and carry waste up and off with you (the old "bag toss" is now illegal in many areas).

• **USE EXISTING TRAILS** Cutting switchbacks causes erosion. When walking off-trail, tread lightly, especially in the desert where cryptogamic soils (usually a dark crust) take thousands of years to form and are easily damaged. Be aware that "rim ecologies" (the clifftop) are often highly sensitive to disturbance.

• **BE DISCREET WITH FIXED ANCHORS** *Bolts are controversial and are not a convenience*—don't place 'em unless they are *really* necessary. Camouflage all anchors. Remove unsightly slings from rappel stations (better to use steel chain or welded cold shuts). Bolts sometimes can be used pro-actively to protect fragile resources—consult with your local land manager.

• **RESPECT THE RULES** and speak up when other climbers don't. Expect restrictions in designated wilderness areas, rock art sites, caves, and to protect wildlife, especially nesting birds of prey. *Power drills are illegal in wilderness and all national parks.*

• **PARK AND CAMP IN DESIGNATED AREAS** Some climbing areas require a permit for overnight camping.

• **MAINTAIN A LOW PROFILE** Leave the boom box and day-glo clothing at home—the less climbers are heard and seen, the better.

• **RESPECT PRIVATE PROPERTY** Be courteous to land owners. Don't climb where you're not wanted.

• **JOIN THE ACCESS FUND!** To become a member, make a tax-deductible donation of $25 or more.

The Access Fund

Preserving America's Diverse Climbing Resources
PO Box 17010 Boulder, CO 80308
303.545.6772 • www.accessfund.org